Pick up and run 2
and run assemblies

Fifteen more easy assemblies for primary schools:
minimum preparation, maximum effect!

Nick Harding

kevin
mayhew

First published in 2005 by

KEVIN MAYHEW LTD
Buxhall, Stowmarket, Suffolk, IP14 3BW
E-mail: info@kevinmayhewltd.com

Some of these assemblies were first published by First
and Best in Education Ltd, Earlstrees Court, Earlstrees
Road, Corby, Northants, NN17 4AX.

9 8 7 6 5 4 3 2 1

ISBN 978 184417 337 2
Catalogue No. 1500752

Edited by Graham Harris
Cover design by Angela Selfe
Typeset by Richard Weaver

Printed and bound in Great Britain

Contents

Each assembly has an object to focus on	Using the object, you can then explore the theme
Introduction	 5
Object	**Theme**
1 *Clock*	New Year 7
2 *Football*	Harvest 11
3 *Toy sword*	St George 13
4 *Suitcase*	St Patrick 17
5 *Letter*	St Andrew 21
6 *Leek*	St David 25
7 *Mattress*	Holidays 29
8 *Towel*	Celebrations 33
9 *Balloons*	Testing times 37
10 *Dictionary*	School year 41
11 *Brick*	Safe places 45
12 *Photo album*	Moving on 49
13 *Bowl of water*	Welcoming 53
14 *Mirror*	Just as we are 57
15 *Cotton*	Work together 61

Introduction

Teachers have a busy time, so there's not always the opportunity to be creative and original in assemblies. This collection aims to give teachers assembly outlines that require minimum preparation but really do get a maximum response.

And so we enter a world of saints, clocks, mattresses and a football! All of these assemblies help to keep things straightforward for teachers, while at the same time giving pupils a great and memorable experience.

Object: Clock
Theme: **New year**

1

Theme	New year, an opportunity to make new starts.
You will need	A clock.
Introduction	What did you do during those strange days between Christmas and New Year? They are such funny times, when Christmas presents break, when the weather seems to be dull and grey from dawn to dusk, and when there is nothing at all to do. How many of you had fights or arguments with your brothers or sisters over the holiday? I expect you all did, really!
	After those strange few days after Christmas Day comes New Year, a time of celebration. Though it is traditional to have a party and to enjoy being together with friends and family at New Year there is real importance to the turning of the year, when one year finishes and another one begins . . . time goes on!
Game	Invite two children to come out, and give each a piece of paper and a pencil. Then allow them one minute to write down as many things to do with the following subjects as possible, stopping after each one to see how they are doing and decide on the best or most original.

- Winter
- Time
- Seasons
- New Year
- Clock
- Watch

Talk The Bible tells us lots about Moses and the people he led, the Israelites. Once they had amazingly escaped from being slaves and servants in Egypt God set them a challenge – to remember the date and celebrate it for all time. But it wouldn't only be a celebration of the good news, as the people had left behind their homes, friends, and the only place they knew. Rather, it was a celebration of what God had done, was doing, and would do, despite the problems and struggles that were being faced.

Story *Kerry's worries*

Kerry looked miserable as she watched the boring TV programmes on New Year's Eve. Dad was in the kitchen doing some jobs, and her mum was out at work, as always. Not only did Kerry feel fed up, she was in trouble too. She'd broken the game she'd been given at Christmas, and she always seemed to be doing things that made her dad mad.

On TV the cheerful presenter was talking about the programmes later that day, New Year's Eve, and wished everyone a Happy New Year. 'I hate life,' she said out loud, 'and I hated this year, and I'll hate next. Everything always goes wrong!' A moment later her dad walked in just as Kerry thumped the cushions on her chair and started to cry.

It took Kerry's dad a long time to work out what was the matter with her, but finally she explained. 'It always goes wrong,' she said, snuffling and wiping her eyes. 'This year I've always been in trouble, and you lost your job, and Mum's at work a lot of the time and really bad-tempered when she's at home, and my report from school was bad, and it's all my fault!'

Her dad sat quietly thinking for a few minutes, and then he said: 'I know it's been a bad year, and you're right, things have gone wrong for you, and they were not all your fault. Your mum and I have tried hard to make it OK, and it's been bad for us too, you know! But as we look back we've got some good things to think about, too. We've still got this house to live in, and your mum's got a job, and we've got the most important thing of all – each other.' Kerry wasn't too sure, but she smiled at her dad as he continued: 'Now, we've got to stick together and look forward.'

Her dad explained: 'The start of a new year is the best time for a new start – why leave it? I'm really going to try to get another job. Your mum's going to try not to be so bad-tempered. And you've got to think about your new starts too. Now's your chance.'

Kerry had a think, and decided to try a bit harder at school, and to be a little tidier at home. The next morning she got up, looked at the clock on her shelf, and said to herself: 'New Year, now's the time for a new start. The new year might not be so bad after all.' **,**

Closing | *Hold up the clock*

Clocks tell us the time, which is always passing. Now's as good a time as any to do the things you should do, and make a new start.

Cover the clock

We can hide the clock, but we can't ignore time passing. The new year will soon be passing quickly, and the chance for change will have passed.

Change the time

We can't put the clock back – what has passed is gone, now we should start to look to the future.

Close your eyes, and think about the good and bad things of last year . . . (*pause*) now think about the new starts you need so that you can make the most of the new year.

Object: Football

Theme: **Harvest**

2

Theme	The world and everything in it!
You will need	A football.
Introduction	Let's do some exercises! First of all breathe in . . . and out . . . and in . . . (*repeat a few times*). Now look all around this hall. Look at the people, the colours, the decorations and displays. Now close your eyes and think of all the food and drink you enjoy. Now stand up . . . run on the spot . . . jump up and down . . . (etc.).
	I wonder if you struggle to get out of bed in the morning? You lie there, listening to the noises around you and hearing your dad call you to get up over and over again. You are so cosy and warm, and feel too tired to move. But life's really good – it's not worth missing by lying around in bed!
Talk	(*Hide the football behind your back.*) At one time the world didn't exist at all. There was nothing here. There was nothing anywhere. (*Move the football around in front of you.*) Then God decided to make the world, round and smooth like this football. At that time it had nothing growing and living – it had no life. But it had been made. But that wasn't the end of the story – God had more plans.
	This football is of no use unless it is used. That was God's next gift to the world – he made life. (*Bounce the ball around.*) He made life by putting fish in water. He made life by creating trees and

11

plants. He made life by making animals and people. He brought the world to life. So here is the world (*hold up the ball*), created by God with life, fish, animals, and people. Then there was food. Who can think of round-shaped food? (*Invite suggestions.*) We have so much to choose from, all growing in the world that God made, all part of his plan, all given life by God.

Activity   Ask the children the following questions, explaining that if their answer is 'yes' they have to stand as quickly as they can:
1. Who has ever spent a whole day without food?
2. Who had breakfast this morning?
3. Who will have at least three meals today?
4. Who has seen pictures of starving people?
5. Who has ever wasted food?
6. Who thinks that people across the world are fair?

Closing   Daily we have food, drink, and life. We can eat and we can enjoy life. It isn't likely that we will ever have to worry about where the next meal is coming from. At Harvest we celebrate God's gifts. It's not just the time to remember farmers growing things in the fields. It's also about the world, and remembering those who suffer. The football reminds us of the world, of the life that God gives to everyone, and the food that he provides.

Prayer   Teach the children this response, to be said after each line:
Thank you, God, for everything.

Thank you, God, for the world you made for us . . .
Thank you, God, for the life in your world . . .
Thank you, God, for the life you have given all of us . . .
Thank you, God, for the food we enjoy . . .
Thank you, God, for all the things you give us . . .

Object: Toy sword
Theme: St George

3

Theme	St George's Day – the fight of good against bad.
You will need	A toy sword.
Story one	*Rob and Nick* ❛Two boys called Rob and Nick were the best of friends. They had been in the same class from the first day, and spent lots of time playing together. They went to each other's houses, and on trips together. But one day it all changed! It started over an argument about who owned a *Smarties* pencil case . . . and it ended in a fight. There in the school corridor Rob and Nick were fighting, until their teacher found them, and gave them a good telling off! ❜
Introduction	It's wrong to fight each other, and you know that at school you mustn't fight. But there are things that need fighting against with words and with actions . . . but not with fists!
Activity	*Swords* Hold up the sword, and wave it around a few times. Ask the children the following questions about it: • If this were real, would it be heavy?

- Who do you know from history who used a sword to fight?
- What piece of armour can you wear to protect yourself from a sword?
- Where are swords worn? What in?

Story two | *St George*

St George is the patron saint of England, of soldiers, and of scouts. It isn't really known why George was chosen as the English patron saint, as he lived in Palestine where Jesus came from, not in Britain. He is believed to have always fought for good and against evil people, and on that one particular famous occasion, against a dragon. He was put to death by some bad people sometime around AD 250.

There was a village in a valley, surrounded by hills and caves. In one of those caves lived a monster, like a dinosaur or dragon, who terrorised the villagers. Each week the creature would go down the hillside to a spot near the village where the villagers put food for it to eat. As the years went on the people remained very scared of the dragon, and would hide in their houses whenever it came near. But they weren't hurt by it – they just put the food out, and waited until it went back to its cave. As long as it was fed it was happy, but what if the food ever ran out?

Then there was a very bad year, when the weather had been too dry and the crops in the fields around the villages had not grown properly. The wheat was thin and dry, the apples were small and rotten, and there was nothing to feed the hungry sheep and cattle. The villagers did the best they could, but soon ran out of food for themselves . . . and for the dragon.

The next time the dragon came for its food there was nothing there, and it grew very angry indeed. In a panic the leaders of the village grabbed a girl from a nearby house and tied her up on a tree near the village. There was no food left, there were no animals to give – she would be food for the dragon, and next week another of the villagers would have to be fed to it. The girl tried to escape, to run away and hide, but it was no good, the ropes were too tight. As soon as the dragon saw her it started to think: 'Yummy . . . dinner', and headed towards her, fire bursting from its nostrils.

Suddenly the dragon stopped and stared into the distance as a man came charging towards it on a horse. The man was a soldier in full armour, and carrying a big, heavy sword. In a flash the sword struck the dragon, who snarled and whipped its tail round to hit the man. All the villagers watched from behind their curtains, hoping that this stranger might just win. The battle went on for a long time and the girl watched as George struck the dragon again and again, while it turned and sent flames towards him. Finally the last stab was delivered, and the dragon slowed down, growled, and slumped to the floor . . . dead!

St George got off his horse and ran to the girl, who was shocked but safe now. He carried her back to the village square, where all the people crowded around, cheering and shouting their thanks. St George had saved the girl, saved the day, and saved the village. **⟩**

Closing St George fought the evil of the dragon. He did what was right, and good won! There are things in school that we all need to fight, not with swords or weapons, but by what we do. We must fight bullies by telling others about them. We must fight people who cause trouble or who say unkind things by ignoring them. We must fight anyone who lets us all down by showing how things should be. Then good will win over bad at school, too!

Prayer Thank you, God, that you helped good St George to save the village. Help us all to fight bad things by trusting you, and doing good. Amen.

Object: Suitcase
Theme: **St Patrick**

4

Theme	St Patrick – journeying through life.
You will need	A suitcase.
Introduction	Who likes to go on journeys? Who has been on holiday lately? Where have you been? (*Allow a little time to ask a few children about their journey experiences.*)

When you go on holiday or on a long journey you have to decide what to take with you. You may want to fill the suitcase with all your favourite toys and games, or lots of videos to watch. You might want to take all your best and trendiest clothes so that you can look cool when you are away! Some people want to take everything in the house away with them. Have your family ever argued about what to take away on holiday?

In a few minutes we are going to listen to a story about a man who travelled a lot, but who took no bags or suitcases with him – he took only his faith in God! |
| **Game** | *Packing*

Invite two pairs of children out to the front. Explain that they must imagine that they are about to go on holiday, and must think of one thing to put in their suitcase beginning with the letter you tell them. The winning pair is the one which comes up with suggestions quickest. |

Examples:

J – jumpers	S – sunglasses	T – towel
B – books	F – food	etc.

Story | *St Patrick*

Teach this response:

Leader: But what did he take?

All: He took only his faith!

This story is about the patron saint of Ireland, St Patrick.

He lived many hundreds of years ago, when travelling was really hard. There were no ferries, trains, buses or aeroplanes. No suitcases or backpacks. Yet St Patrick travelled to many places. But what did he take? *He took only his faith!*

Most of us travel to go on holiday or to make visits to people or interesting places. But St Patrick's first long journey was not by choice. Patrick grew up in Scotland, where he learned to trust God for everything, and became a strong young man. Then one day he was attacked by a group of thieves who hated Christians like him. They kidnapped Patrick and took him on a boat to Ireland. But what did he take? *He took only his faith!*

When he arrived in Ireland he had no money and didn't know anyone, so he had to do the work that his kidnappers gave him. He ended up feeding pigs and cattle on a farm. It was smelly, dirty work and Patrick hated it. But even though he was really lonely and sad not to be at home he still trusted God, and prayed that God would sort it out.

One day Patrick got the opportunity to escape from the awful farm. The others were not around, so he left everything behind him and headed off to the coast. But what did he take? *He took only his faith*! After days of walking he got to a port, and hoped to find a boat to take him back to his home in Scotland. But as he prayed he felt God tell him to get on another one instead, and he finally ended up sailing to France. But what did he take? *He took only his faith*!

Once in France Patrick found some men who trusted God – monks – and they helped him learn more. He was happy at last, and felt at home with them. But again he knew that God wanted him to move on, so he set off for another boat. He really wanted to go back to Scotland, but he knew he should go and tell the people of Ireland about God instead. So he boarded another boat, and returned to Ireland. But what did he take? *He took only his faith*!

In Ireland Patrick became famous, and travelled around talking to kings and queens, farmers and poor people, about God. Everywhere he went people wanted to know more, and he helped lots of people learn more about God. But what did he take? *He took only his faith*!

Closing

When we travel we take a suitcase or bag like this one. We fill it with all the things we need, we want, and we think we want. Yet

St Patrick took only one thing – his faith in God. He knew that God is always there, God will always help, and God will give all the things you need.

Object: Letter

Theme: **St Andrew**

Theme	St Andrew – real friends.
You will need	A letter.
Introduction	Who has friends? Who thinks that they are a good friend for other people? We all need friends, and we all have friends. Your brothers or sisters have friends, and your parents have friends. Even your teachers have friends!
Story: part one	*Jesus chooses friends*

'As Jesus walked along the shore of the Sea of Galilee he watched the fishermen out on their boats as usual. He saw those that he knew well and the others as they cast their nets over the side and then haul them in, full of fresh fish.

As he wandered along he saw Andrew, the brother of Simon. He was sitting on the edge of his boat mending some nets. Jesus knew that he was going to have lots of work to do and people to help, and he needed some friends to go with him.

'Andrew,' said Jesus, 'will you be one of my special friends? Will you come with me and help others?'

21

Game | *Fun Friends*

Invite two really good friends to the front, and send one out of the hall. Then ask the other one some of the following questions before inviting the first one back and asking them the same questions about themself. If the answers are the same they get a big round of applause, if wrong a sigh from everyone!

- What is your friend's worst habit?
- What does your friend get really angry about?
- What does your friend really like to eat?
- What is your friend's favourite TV programme?
- Who else lives in the home of your friend?
- Where would your friend love to go to on holiday?

Story: part two | *Jesus' arguing friends*

'It was some months later, and Andrew the fisherman was one of Jesus' special friends who went with him and helped him. They had seen some amazing things. They had seen Jesus make a blind man see, and a lame man walk. They had heard him speak to 5000 people and make enough food appear for them all.

They were walking from one village to another when the friends started to argue, like friends do. Andrew and the others all wanted to know if they were Jesus' favourite friend, and they were getting really angry with each other. Jesus calmed them down, and explained: 'I don't have favourites, I love everyone the same. You are my friends, and I am yours.' Andrew and the other friends of Jesus thought about it, and tried to be better friends after that. '

Illustration | *Letter*

I have a letter here, and I think it's from a good friend of mine. I don't see them as often as I would like to, but we do keep in touch by writing letters. Let's see what it says.

> Dear . . . . How are you? It was really good to hear about all the things you are doing from your last letter. Those children at your school sound really horrible!
>
> I am fine now, after recovering from the flu. I'm really pleased that I have a friend like you, because I can trust you and call on you for help. Thank you for being there for me.
>
> Bye for now, ...

Well, that was a really nice letter. They are a really good friend to me too, and I suppose that's what friendship should be all about. I do things for them, and they do things for me.

Story: part three | *Jesus leaves his friends*

Jesus had gone! His friends had seen him die, and had been amazed when he came alive again. Now he had gone up to heaven, and they were on their own. Andrew and the others knew that now was the time when they must be really good friends. They would have to stick together and help each other, as they set out to tell others about Jesus and the amazing things that he had done.

They started to have services and times to pray, and they shared all they had with each other. As more people saw what good friends Jesus' friends were they came along to find out more.

23

Closing | We all need friends. We rely on them, and we gain so much by being a friend for someone else. Of course, friends are not always noticed. They are often the sort of people who quietly help and support, and don't need or even want to draw lots of attention to themselves.

Andrew, the very first disciple to be called by Jesus, was an ordinary man. Like Jesus' other friends, he introduced others to Jesus, and he was always there, always reliable . . . a true friend. The life of St Andrew, patron saint of Scotland, Russia and fishermen, may help us all to be better friends.

Prayer | Sit quietly and picture the face of your best friend in your mind. Think about all the things you do together, and how good it is to have a friend. Thank God in your heart for all your friends.

Object: Leek
Theme: **St David**

6

Theme	St David – living the simple life.
You will need	A leek.
Introduction	If we make a meal we need ingredients. Perhaps we have meat, vegetables, water, gravy, or other things. Every day has ingredients too – we get up, have breakfast, get changed, come to school, and so on. Every day is busy . . . perhaps too busy! How many of you go to Cub Scouts, or Brownies? How many of you go horseriding or dancing? We have so much to do that sometimes there is no time to stop and be quiet.
Activity	*Day mimes* Encourage the children to sit and work in pairs. One of the pair must mime all the things they do in a day, without using any speech or sound effects. If it works without too much noise swop over, and let the other one of each pair have a go.
Story	*St David* (*Hold up the leek.*) This is a symbol of the Welsh nation, and some people wear them on St David's Day. But who was St David, and what did he do?

25

Hundreds of years ago a very religious lady called Non married a Welsh chieftain. They lived many miles away from the nearest town, and lived a very simple life. After a few years they had a son and called him David; he grew up with them on their land. As he grew older David worked on the land with his parents, growing crops and looking after animals. They lived simply, ate basic food like leeks, potatoes and bread, and worshipped God.

David was really interested in Christianity, and when he was old enough he moved to live with some monks – holy men who spent time praying and growing food for themselves. David proved to be a quick learner, and before long he was teaching and telling others about Jesus. Like his parents, he believed in living simply, and only allowed himself to eat vegetables like potatoes and leeks. He spent as much time as possible praying and learning more about Jesus.

As he got older David decided that it was important to set up more monasteries – homes for monks – and he started to build some in Wales and England. David and his monks would work on each monastery themselves every day. There was a time when a robber tried to scare David away by damaging the building every night, but instead of getting angry David just worked harder. Finally the robber gave up, and joined the monastery instead of working against it.

By the time he died David had set up 12

monasteries around Wales and England. In them the monks lived basically, concentrating on growing simple food for themselves, and using the rest of the time in prayer. Through all his hard work many more people learned about God's love for them, and how to live a simple life. 🌙

Illustration

Leek soup

Hold up the leek. Ask the children to close their eyes and think for 30 seconds about what you will need to get to make leek soup. Then take suggestions.

Leek soup is very simple to make – it doesn't need complicated ingredients or lots of hard work. It is possibly one of the easiest soups to make. All you have to do is chop up the leek, add lots of water, and boil it for about 30 minutes. The ingredients are simple – just water and leeks!

In life it's good to have lots of ingredients – things to do, people to see, activities and fun. But sometimes it's good to keep things simple and uncomplicated. David wanted people to live simple lives rather than get too complicated. That's important for us, too.

Prayer

Let's spend some time in quiet.

Thank you, God, for all you do for us. Help us not to get so busy that we forget you. Help us to live simple lives. Amen.

Object: Mattress

Theme: **Holidays**

7

Theme | Holidays – time to rest and relax.

You will need | A mattress or bean bag.

Story one | *Simon*

(*Start by lying on the mattress or bean bag and snoring. Act out the story as much as you like as you tell it.*)

Simon woke up, yawned, and nearly went to sleep again! He didn't like having to get up, but the light was streaming through the window into the house, and he could see that his parents and sister had already got up and gone.

Simon lived in Judaea at around the time that Jesus lived. The family house was square, with one room inside and some steps up the outside onto the flat roof. Most days Simon would get up early to help his father in his fields before going to spend a few hours in the temple learning from the teachers there.

It took a while for Simon to work out that today was different – it was one of the special holy days. Quickly he got up, went outside to the well to wash, and found his parents. 'I'm glad you've got up at last,' said his mother, with a kindly smile. 'It's time to go to the temple for the service.' On holy days all the people in a village or area would go to the temple to remember God, and the good things he has done for them. For the rest of the day they would spend time at home, talking and having fun rather than working or cooking.

Simon sat through the service in the temple, which was as long as usual! Then they went home, and spent the rest of the day walking in the fields, talking and playing. He didn't usually see much of his parents, because they worked so hard to grow crops. Holy days were very special days for Simon. 〟

Talk These days we call them holidays. In Simon's time many hundreds of years ago they were called holy days, special days put aside for God and family. Whatever we call them, it is important to spend time having a rest, getting refreshed, and enjoying time with friends and family.

Activity *Holidays*

Invite three children to the front. Ask them each to speak on one of the following subjects for 15 seconds without stopping. Ask the children to cheer for the speaker they think does best.

- Drinking a can of cold cola
- Having cool shower on a hot day
- Going swimming on the beach
- A lovely long walk in the country
- Eating lots of ice creams
- A long lie-in that lasts all day!

Story two | *Becky's holiday*

❝Becky was looking forward to her holidays from school. As the last afternoon of term passed by she kept looking at the clock, and felt really excited. The bell rang, Mr Turner told them to put their chairs up, and off she went.

Becky ran home and started to pack. It was going to be the best holiday ever. When Bill, her step-dad, came home from work he had a quick cup of tea and then said: 'Right, Becky, let's get going.' Soon they were heading down the motorway to the Little Chef restaurant where Becky would be meeting her dad. The road was busy, the traffic was slow, but finally they got there.

(*Sit or lie on the mattress.*) By bedtime Becky was tucked up in bed in her dad's new house. She was really happy to see him again – she did miss him. Over the next few days she had lots of long lie-ins, and went for walks holding hands with her dad. It rained most of the time, and there were no places to visit. But it was a great holiday despite the weather – holidays were very special for Becky. ❞

Talk | God designed us to have holidays! After he had created the world he took a day off to rest and get refreshed. We need holidays so that we can do our best the rest of the time. Your teachers need holidays to sleep!

You might spend this holiday seeing people you don't usually see, like Becky did going to stay with her dad. You might spend it having long lie-ins on a comfy bed like this one, or sleeping on a hot, sunny beach. You might enjoy having more time with

31

your brothers or sisters, and parents, like Simon did in our first story.

Whatever you do this holiday make the most of it, and enjoy yourself!

Object: **Towel**

Theme: **Celebrations**

Theme | Life is full of celebrations.

You will need | One white towel.

Introduction | I wonder how many of you have been to a celebration lately? You might have been to a birthday party, a wedding, or some other celebration. Who has a birthday today? Come out! (*Sing 'Happy Birthday' and make a fuss of the birthday child/children.*)

Talk | Get two volunteers out to the front. Give one the towel and ask them to wear it like a nappy! Encourage all the children to cry like babies (*Waaaa!*) whenever you say: 'When a baby is born . . .'

Life is full of celebrations. From the moment a baby is born (*Waaaa!*) there are celebrations. After months of waiting and preparation before the baby is born (*Waaa!*), buying special baby things, painting a room, and sorting everything out, the baby is born (*Waaaa!*). People have a celebration while the baby cries, poos and is sick everywhere! The proud parents show off the baby after it is born (*Waaaa!*). Grandparents, aunts and uncles, brothers and sisters all come to visit. Everyone has something to celebrate after a baby is born (*Waaaa!*).

Pass the towel to the other volunteer, and ask them to wave it like a flag when the children shout Hurray! Encourage all the children to respond with Hurray! when you say 'things to celebrate'.

33

As you get older there are more things to celebrate (*Hurray!*). Things to celebrate (*Hurray!*) include birthdays, which come round for each of us every year. There is also Christmas and New Year, and there are anniversaries and weddings. There are other things to celebrate (*Hurray!*) as you get older. You might be successful in an exam or test. You might get a girlfriend or a boyfriend! Lots of things to celebrate (*Hurray!*) come as you get older with a new job, your own wedding . . . and your own children. From the moment a baby is born (*Waaa!*) right through life there are things to celebrate (*Hurray!*).

Story   *Joshua and the river*

Ask a volunteer out to act the part of Joshua, wearing the towel on his/her head.

Joshua was the leader of God's people, and after a long journey lasting many years they were nearly home at last. The people cheered, sang songs and danced in celebration as they looked from the hilltop to see ahead a really good land, full of trees and streams, ideal for them to live in.

As Josh led the people over the rocky land towards it they started to see something glistening in the hot sunlight. Once they drew closer they realised it was a very wide river, with no bridges, and no way to cross. It was too deep to wade through, and flowing too fast to swim across. The celebrations stopped, and they began to cry out in despair: 'Are we ever going to get over that river? Are we ever going to reach that wonderful land?' Joshua looked worried. What could they do? He could think of no way to cross it, but he knew God would help. Joshua walked a little way away from the crowd of people, and prayed. As he knelt he knew what God was saying, so he called all the people together and told them what to do. 'God wants us to cross the river and celebrate,' he said. 'Today, I want you to rest and pray, and tomorrow we will walk into the river and the water will stop flowing!'

The people were amazed, and some thought it was a silly idea. Many were scared that they would be washed away by the water. But they so much wanted to get to their new land that they did as he said.

The next day Joshua shouted: 'Get ready!' and the people lined up ready to cross the fast-flowing, deep and dangerous river. As the first ones stepped into the water the people gasped to see it stop, and they all crossed safely. They ran like little children onto the dry land on the other side – their land. For days they sang, danced, prayed, feasted, and celebrated! ❜

Closing Celebrations happen all the time, remembering the good things in life. God has given us so much. It's good to celebrate all that we have and all that we are, from the moment we are born as babies, and all through our lives.

Object: Balloons
Theme: Testing times

9

Theme	Tests and challenges – doing your best.
You will need	Six balloons.
Introduction	Even many, many years ago, when your teachers were at school, they had to do tests! They had to learn lots of things beforehand, and then try to remember it all on the day. They know what it feels like to be really worried about it, to feel that they've answered all the questions wrong, and to dread the results and the report to parents!
	But there are other tests and challenges in life, too. There is the driving test. Imagine crashing while the examiner is sitting in the car deciding if you are a good driver or not! There is the challenge of getting a good school report, keeping your bedroom tidy, or running a race.
	Many of us don't really like tests or challenges – we find them scary or hard. But they have to be faced, whether we like it or not!
Game	*Bursting balloons*
	Invite two children out to the front. Give each one a balloon. The challenge is to blow the balloon up, tie it, and then burst it first! You may have to tie them yourself as children often find that quite hard.

37

Story one | *Moses*

> Moses was a man from the Bible. He was an ordinary shepherd, but God chose him to do lots of things for him. On one occasion Moses was leading thousands of people through the desert but they had no water. God said that if Moses hit a nearby rock it would flow with water. Moses didn't know what to do – it was a real test of him. Ask the children: Should he hit the rock and hope that water comes out? Should he carry on and try to find a stream?
>
> Moses took the test. He hit the rock, and water flowed from it so that all the people and their animals could have plenty to drink.

Illustration | Hold up a deflated balloon.

If you don't bother to work hard and do your best in life it will be like this balloon – a bit saggy, weak and useless. There are tests and challenges, but you must at least try to make the most of them.

Story two | *Sir Winston*

> Sir Winston Churchill was Prime Minister of Britain more than 50 years ago, while World War II was being fought. During the war many men went abroad to fight, and many were killed. It cost a lot of money, and families living around here were poor and struggled to get enough food to eat. Ask older members of your family about it. Sir Winston could have given up during the war, and it was very hard for him to keep going. There were times when he felt like

giving up. Ask the children: Should he carry on as leader? Should he give up?

The test was to help the people get through the war, and in the end, after six very hard years for Sir Winston and everyone else, the war was over.

Illustration

If you have a test or a challenge it can seem too much to get through. But if you don't do your best it is like this. (*Blow the balloon half up, and then let it go!*) If you don't face up to the challenge fully and only try a little, then it doesn't work, and it ends up being a waste of time, like this balloon!

Story three

The giant-killer

David was about 13 when the giant called Goliath came to his land and challenged all the soldiers to a fight. No one was brave enough to face up to the test, because Goliath was so big and so strong.

David had been feeding sheep when he saw that the army were all standing around, too scared to fight. He looked up to see the giant towering over them all. He knew that someone had to try to fight, and he had to decide whether to take the challenge or not.

Ask the children: Should he take the test? Or should he leave it to someone else?

David took the test. Armed only with a strip of cloth and two stones he managed to kill the giant.

Illustration

Blow up a balloon and tie it.

If you do your best when you face a test or challenge you will be like this balloon. It now looks good and it is doing what it should be doing! You might not always do brilliantly, but that doesn't matter. The challenges in life are about trying, like David, Sir Winston and Moses did.

Closing Close your eyes and think about all the tests and challenges you face. They might be at school, at home or somewhere else. God helped Moses and David – he will help you do your best if you ask him.

Object: Dictionary

Theme: **School year**

10

Theme	The new school year – learn all you can!
You will need	A school dictionary.
Introduction	Most adults look back on life with a few regrets. Your mums or dads may sometimes think or say things like: 'I wish I had worked a bit harder at school' or 'I wish I had carried on having those piano lessons.' Those who didn't learn to swim while at school regret it, and others think that they would have been better spending more time reading books like this dictionary. School might not seem like fun sometimes, but it is a great place to learn new things, and a new school year is a great time to try a bit harder.
Game	*Which word?* Split all the children into two teams. Hold the dictionary, and explain that it is a book full of words and definitions – descriptions of what the word means. Close your eyes, open the dictionary at random, read out a definition, and ask one of the teams to tell you the word. If they can't, ask the other team instead. Repeat it a few times, awarding points to the successful team each time.

Story | *Jesus learns*

Jesus grew up in the home of Mary and Joseph. Joseph was a carpenter, and it's likely that Jesus would have helped him sometimes, learning how to look after wood and make things well. But Jesus also spent some time at school. The schools were run in the temples, like churches, and teachers explained about words, writing, and about God to the children who wanted to learn more. Jesus would have gone to school like many of the other children, and made the most of his chance to learn.

Once a year all of the people in Jesus' village went away for a few days to Jerusalem for a celebration. Mary and Joseph took Jesus, and they all had a good time. As they were on their way home Mary suddenly said to Joseph: 'Where's Jesus? Is he with you?' Joseph couldn't see him anywhere, and realised that Jesus was nowhere to be seen. 'We'll have to go back to Jerusalem to find him,' he said.

Mary and Joseph were very worried as they rushed back along the dusty road to the city. Where could Jesus be? They started to search the rooms where they had stayed, and the roads nearby. After looking for many hours they decided to have a rest in the temple, when they spotted him there, sitting on the floor talking to the priests. As they went closer they heard Jesus asking questions, finding out as much as he could, listening and learning all the time. The priests were really impressed with all that Jesus knew, and his eagerness to learn more. As Mary and Joseph set off back home with Jesus they asked him why he had been there. 'Didn't you realise that I would be there!' he said. **❜**

Activity

All the children need to stand, and learn this rap from the Bible (Proverbs 19:8):

'Do yourself a favour and learn all you can.'

Then say the rap in a number of different ways, such as shouting, whispering, loud, quiet, clicking fingers, clapping, stamping feet, silent miming, etc.

Closing

Even the Bible encourages us to do all we can to learn. School is the best place to learn about maths and history, science and art, and all the other things that we do here. But we also learn how to be kind, how to look after each other, and how to behave. This school year we all need to do ourselves a favour and learn all we can.

Prayer

Father God, thank you for this school. Thank you for all the teachers, cleaners, and other helpers who work here. Thank you for all the children who learn here. Help us all to think more, listen more, and learn more this year. Amen.

Object: Brick

Theme: Safe places

11

Theme	It is good to know that there are safe places to go to.
You will need	A brick.
Game	*Buildings* Invite two teams of three volunteers out to the front. Explain that each team has to think of a different type of building in turn. The team that hesitates too long or repeats a type of building that has already been said is out of the game. The types of buildings are things like church, school, house, bank, shop, etc.
Introduction	This brick is not doing much, but there are bricks around us all the time. When bricks are put together they make buildings, and we use many buildings. Some of the buildings we use are safe places, where we can have a good time and feel safe. Imagine what it would be like to have nowhere to go, and nowhere to live. You would feel lonely and lost, and not at all safe.
Story one	*The two ladies* In a large town in England lived two ladies. They were not rich or famous, they were just ordinary like you or me. One evening they went

45

out to visit friends, and on the way back noticed that there were some people settling down to sleep on the streets and doorways of shops. For the next few days and weeks they couldn't settle – they were really concerned about those people who had nowhere safe to go.

The two ladies started to talk to the important people in the town, raised money, saved up, and eventually bought a small house. In it they decorated the rooms and moved beds in. Then they opened it up for any homeless people to visit and sleep in. The people the two ladies had seen sleeping on the streets had a safe place to go to at last! **"**

Quiz | *Safe places*

Split all the children into two teams, and describe a safe place to each team in turn using the given clues. Award more points the less clues the team needs.

Castle   Often built on a hill
Made out of stone
Safe place to fight battles from

School   Lots of people go there
It is a place to learn in
You are all in one now!

Home   Where you can go to rest
You may have your own room in it
It is where you spend time with your family

Church   There are lots of them
They are often tall, some have towers
They are always used on Sundays, and other days too

Story two | *Hannah's son*

> Hannah was very sad. She was getting older, and she and her husband really wanted to have a child, but they never had. She would often go to a place where she felt safe – a temple. There she would spend hours praying and crying, asking God to allow her to have a child.
>
> After all those years of sadness and upset she found that she was expecting a baby, and she was thrilled! She told the priest in the temple, and all her friends and family. Some of them didn't believe her! Eventually the baby was born, and it was a boy. She wanted the very best for him after all the time she had waited and she wanted him to be safe always. She decided that when he was old enough she would take him to live at the church or temple. She knew he would be safe there.
>
> Hannah's son was called Samuel, and when he had grown she took him to meet the priest Eli, and handed him over. She promised to visit him often, and knew that he would be safe in the temple – it was a safe place.
>
> Samuel learned a lot from Eli, who taught him how to read and write. In return Samuel helped Eli do all sorts of jobs around the church. As he grew he knew that he was in a safe place. Later he became one of God's special messengers, and did lots of good things.

Closing | Where is your favourite safe place? You might really like going into your bedroom away from everyone. You might like to sit at one particular table in your classroom.

We all have safe places where we can go. But wherever we are we can be sure that God is with us and will keep us safe. We don't need to be surrounded by bricks like this one to be safe!

Object: Photo album
Theme: **Moving on**

12

Theme	Moving on is not as hard as it seems.
You will need	A photograph album.
Introduction	Who has a photograph album like this one? What sort of pictures do you put in it?

In most photo albums there are pictures from the past. There may be pictures taken on a holiday or when visiting friends, pictures of babies and pets. There are likely to be many pictures which bring back memories of the past.

Older people, like your teachers and parents, tend to say things like: 'Oh, I remember when . . .' and: 'In my day . . .' a lot! They think back to the past and remember good times and bad times, nice places and nasty places, before they moved on to wherever they went next.

Game

Posing photos

Invite two teams of four people out to the front. The idea of the game is for them to get into a still pose as if they are in a photograph. You will give them the topic, and the other children, by clapping loudest, will choose which team they think makes the best photo.

- A posed family photo including a baby
- A photo of lazy days on the beach

- A photo of the family having an argument
- A photo taken at a disco
- A photo taken in the playground
- A photo taken at Christmas dinner

Story one | *Katie's fear*

Before the summer holidays Katie just couldn't get to sleep. She would lie in bed looking through the photos of her classmates at school, and think back to all the good times. As the holidays came closer the more she dreaded leaving her school and going on to the bigger one, with lots of teachers and children, in the next village.

Katie had been at the same school since she was 4, and now she was 11. She had got used to all the same friends every day, many of whom had always been in the same class as her. She was used to the teachers, the dinner ladies, even the caretaker. As she lay awake she felt like crying and her heart thumped. It just wouldn't be the same at the next school, and she didn't want to move on.

Six months later Katie was tidying up her bedroom when she found the photo album under her bed. She opened it and glanced at the pictures. Some of the memories came back, but she didn't really miss the old village school at all. It hadn't taken her long to get used to the bigger school with bigger rooms and more teachers. She had found some of her old friends there, and made new friends. As she closed the photo album and thought back to those sleepless nights she said to herself: 'Moving on wasn't so bad after all!' **"**

Story two | *Ruth starts again*

" Things had been hard for Ruth. She had met a man years before and they had got married. For a while it had all gone well, and the small farm they had produced enough food for them and a little to sell, too. But then tragedy had struck, and her husband died. Ruth did all she could to get by without him, but a few years without any rain followed and the farm could no longer produce enough food.

One evening Ruth and her friend Naomi sat by a fire and talked. There was no hope where they were – there was no food anywhere, and if they stayed they would die. It was time to move on.

They set out on a journey, but they weren't sure where they would end up. Naomi had some relatives and they decided to try there first. When they arrived, tired and thin after many weeks walking, they were made very welcome.

Before long Ruth and Naomi were settled in their new homes, and they often thought back to the hard times they had left behind. They were glad they had moved on. **"**

Closing | Life contains lots of changes, and times to move on. Many of you have moved house and school in the past, and all of you will in the next few years. Moving on is not as hard or painful as you may think, and it is exciting to have new challenges and new opportunities. As you look back, like flicking through an old photo album, you will have good memories. But once you have moved on those times have passed and new times have replaced them. It's good to move on!

Prayer

Father God, be with us all as we move on. Help us to look back and remember the good times we have had. Help us to look forward to the good times we will have. Help us not to fear what is ahead, or yearn for what has gone. Amen.

Object: Bowl of water
Theme: **Welcoming**

13

Theme | Welcoming people.

You will need | A bowl of water.

Introduction | Can you remember what it's like to be new to somewhere? Once, not that many months ago, you were all new at school. Do you remember what it was like that first day? All the children arrived feeling a little bit scared or worried. Their mums or dads brought them and looked as worried as the children.

Once in the classroom the new children soon settled in. The teachers made them feel welcome by looking after them and cheering them up. The older children who had been in school longer made the new ones feel welcome by looking after them at playtime and showing them around.

It is hard to go somewhere new, but it's made a lot easier if someone makes you feel welcome!

Story | *Elijah is welcome – part one*

Have three children out to play the parts of Elijah, Sarah and her son. Encourage them to say the spoken sections by repeating the phrases after you.

Elijah was a poor man, but a special one too. He was a traveller who went from town to town and village to village telling people about God.

53

Some people made him welcome by giving him food and a place to sleep, but in other places no one made him welcome at all. One day Elijah was not sure what to do next, so he sat down and said: 'God, what shall I do?' As usual he knew that God was telling him where to go now, and he set off on his journey to the next town. After a long walk in the sunshine he saw the houses clustered ahead, and he looked forward to finding somewhere to rest.

In the town Sarah and her son were talking. 'What are we going to do?' she said. 'I don't know,' said the boy. They were very poor, they didn't have much food, and Sarah's husband, the boy's dad, had died some years before. Now they only had a tiny bit of flour left, which she was going to use to make one last loaf of bread. In the end Sarah decided to go off to the well in the middle of the village and get some water – at least they could have a drink. **"**

Illustration

In the land where Elijah was travelling people made others feel welcome by doing a very strange thing – they washed their feet! (*Invite a few teachers or children to the front, and using the bowl of water wash their feet!*) This was the way to make people feel really welcome. After long, tiring walks wearing sandals on dusty roads the very best thing for visitors and new people was a good wash, especially of the feet.

There are many ways you can make people feel welcome. You can shake hands, offer them somewhere to sit, or make them a drink. You can share food with them, or let them play with your favourite games.

Story | *Elijah is welcome – part two*

❟ As Sarah and her son were collecting water from the well Elijah came up to them. 'Could I have a drink of your water?' he asked. 'What shall I do?' asked the lady to her son. In the end they gave Elijah a drink, and listened to him as he told them all about his work telling people about God. Then he said how hungry he was. Sarah explained that they only had enough food for one meal, but they would share it with him.

As Elijah went through the door into their house Sarah and her son came along with a bowl of water and a towel. She knelt down at Elijah's feet, and washed them. Now Elijah felt really welcome! Then she did some cooking, and they ate the last of the food in the house.

At bedtime Sarah's son wanted some more food, but Sarah reminded him that it was all gone. 'What shall we do?' he asked her. As Elijah settled to sleep on the floor he thought about Sarah and her son, and how much they had done to make him feel welcome. 'God, what shall I do?' he asked.

The next day Sarah went to her kitchen while Elijah and her son talked. Then they heard an excited shout. 'We've got food, we've got food!' she said, as she came running to them. 'God has given you all you need because you made me so welcome,' said Elijah. From then on Sarah always found more food when she went in the kitchen, and she and her son never ran out of things to eat. ❞

Closing It is hard to settle in a new place – it is good to make new people feel welcome. Remember the bowl of water and the washing of feet. We don't have to do that now, but we can make other people feel welcome in our classes, in our school or at home in lots of other ways. Let's all try to make other people feel welcome.

Object: Mirror

Theme: **Just as we are**

14

Theme	God loves us just the way we are.
You will need	A mirror.
Game	*Find the person*

Invite 12 children out to the front. They should be a mixture of all – young, older, tall, short, different coloured hair, and so on. It adds an element of fun if a teacher or two volunteer! Then ask them to go and stand by the person you describe from the list below:

- Hop to the person who has the nicest smile
- Crawl to the person who is really happy
- Dance to the person who looks really fit and healthy
- Limp to the person who has the longest hair
- Tiptoe to the person who wears the brightest clothes
- Hobble to the person who is really old
- Jump to the person who is really young
- March to the person who has long arms
- Slouch to the person who is a bad example!
- Walk to the person who works hard at school

Introduction

If you go along to the main road today you will see lots of cars, but many of them will be the same! Who can tell me the make of a car? And a model of that make? If you were to see two new red

Ford (Mondeo) cars here now they would look exactly the same. The colour would be the same, the lights would be in the same place, the shape would be the same, and the inside would be the same.

We are all different! It is amazing that everyone in the world looks a little different from everyone else, even if they are identical twins. And the difference does not stop with how we look. We all think different things all the time, we all have different abilities, we all have other things which we are not so good at.

Illustration

Turn and look into the face of the person next to you. Look carefully at their hair, their eyes and nose, the shape of their mouth, whether they are smiling or not, and everything else you can see. Take in as much as you can while you are looking.

Now put your hand up if the answer to any of these questions is yes:

- Have they got the same colour hair as you?
- Have they got a nice smile?
- Is their nose the same as yours?
- Do they have freckles?
- Do you think they cleaned their teeth this morning?
- Is their hair curly?

Everyone in this hall, in this school, in this village/town is different, which is amazing!

Story

Tim and the mirror

❝Early one morning, a moment after he had dragged himself out of bed, Tim looked in the mirror. 'Yuk,' he said to himself, as he saw his blotchy red face, hair all messy, and dirty teeth. Tim really didn't like himself. You see, he was

Mirror: **Just as we are**

one of those boys who always looked a mess whatever he wore and however hard he tried to be tidy. He ended up with his trousers creased, his shoes covered in mud, and his hair messed up. Because of how he looked other children would keep away from him, and he had very few friends. Day after day Tim looked at himself in the mirror and wished he could look different.

On his way to school Tim walked along the main road, past the shops. As he walked along on his own, seeing others in small groups chatting and laughing, he felt really alone. Then he saw a car parked, and a man struggling to change a tyre. As he got closer he realised it was Mr Perkins, one of the teachers. 'Can I help, sir?' Tim asked as he got near. 'Oh yes, Tim, if you don't mind. You see, I've got a puncture and I'm changing the wheel.' With Tim's help Mr Perkins soon got going again, and he was very grateful. 'You know, Tim, you're one of the most helpful children at our school,' he said.

During the morning Tim sat on his own – no one else wanted to sit next to a scruffy boy like him! When the dinner bell rang he got his lunch from his bag and headed off to the hall. In the corridor one of the girls from his class, Lucy, tripped over and dropped her lunch box which burst open. Her sandwiches, crisps, apple and yoghurt all ended up scattered over the floor. In a flash Tim was there, picking up the lunch and helping Lucy get back on her feet. 'You are one of the kindest people I know,' she said to him as they ate their lunch together.

When he got home after school that evening Tim was feeling good. He remembered what Mr Perkins and Lucy had said, and he felt really good inside. 'I don't care what people think of how I look,' he said to himself. 'It's what I'm like inside that matters.' And with that he looked in the mirror and smiled. **,**

Closing

We might look in a mirror like this and think 'Yuk' or 'Wow!'. We might want to be better at swimming, really good at maths, brainier than we are. But whatever we think of ourselves God loves us as we are, and he made us that way.

The Bible tells us that God knew us even before we were born, and wanted us to be happy as we are. Let's do our best to enjoy the life we have, just as we are!

Prayer

Thank you, Father God, that you love all of us just as we are. Help us to make the most of the life you give us, and help us to be really happy with ourselves. Amen.

Object: Cotton

Theme: **Work together**

15

Theme	Working together is better than working alone!
You will need	A reel of cotton.
Introduction	Who can tell me what you would need to build a school like this one? You would need bricks, cement and glass. You would need lots of pipes, tubes and wires. But the most important thing of all would be to have people to do the work. Could one man or woman build a school like this? It would take too long! You would need a group of many people to work together, and then the school would get built.
Illustration	On the island of Guernsey, near France, is a little chapel. It is so small that there is only room for a few people to stand in the main room, and the corridors are so low that you have to duck to get through. The chapel is decorated with lots of little shells and pieces of colourful pottery which are pressed into the plaster of the walls inside and outside. The little chapel is really pretty, and gets lots of visitors. But the most unusual thing about the little chapel is that it was built by one man, a monk. It took him all of his life to do it.
	It would have been quicker to get others to help him, and then the chapel would have been finished quicker. But there were no others who wanted to work with him all their lives, so he was left on his own.

Activity | *Building together*

Invite a number of groups of five children to the front, and ask them to make the following shapes using their bodies and working together. They may need a little help.

- A wigwam
- A chocolate-wrapping machine
- A car
- A church with a spire
- A playground slide

They couldn't have done that on their own – they all needed to work together, and then it was possible to make those silly shapes!

Story | *Nehemiah's building*

Nehemiah was a man who lived a very long time ago. We read about him in the Bible.

❛Nehemiah worked for the king in a country a long way away from his own. The king liked him, but Nehemiah often felt homesick and wished he could go back to where he had grown up. One day he heard that his home town, Jerusalem, was in a mess. The walls had been knocked down and many buildings were falling apart. Nehemiah decided that he had to go and try to do something to rebuild Jerusalem.

The next morning he went to the king and explained, and the king was very understanding. He even gave Nehemiah some money to help him. Then he set off on the long journey home. When he got there he saw a real mess. It was much worse than he had imagined. The walls were all collapsing, buildings looked like they had been half knocked down, and there seemed little hope that one man could achieve anything. But Nehemiah soon found that he was not on his own. Before long other people came along to help him, and after many months of hard work the walls, the houses and the whole city was back to how it was in better times. Nehemiah was really grateful for the others who had worked with him. ❞

Illustration

Cotton

(*Take the cotton and break off one long thread. Ask a child out to help you.*)

This cotton thread is very thin. If you were to hang something heavy from it you would find that it would soon break. On its own, as a thin thread of cotton, it isn't much use. (*Ask the child to break the thread, and then take two threads.*)

Now we have two weak threads of cotton. If I twine them together they are not much stronger, yet they are better than one thread. However, if you try hard they will still break. (*Ask the child to break the threads – it is harder, but is possible. Then take three threads.*)

Now we have three weak threads. If I twine them together you may think that they will be nearly as weak as two or one, but that's wrong. Three threads are working together, and no matter how hard you try, you will probably not be able to break them! (*Ask the child to break the three twined threads. They should not be able to!*)

Closing

One thread wasn't much use on its own. One man wasn't going to rebuild Jerusalem. But as other threads were added the twine became unbreakable, and as other people helped the walls were rebuilt.

In life there are lots of times when you need to work together. At home it's so much better if everyone does their bit and keeps things clean and tidy. If you are playing a game of football or netball you need others to help – you can't do it all on your own. At school we will never keep it a really happy, safe, fun place to be unless we all work together. If we do we will be unbreakable, just like the cotton!